Student's Book

58 St Aldates
Oxford
OX1 1ST
United Kingdom

Beep Student's Book / Activity Book Level 4

First Edition: 2014
Eleventh Reprint: February 2018
ISBN: 978-607-06-0920-6

© Text: Brendan Dunne, Robin Newton
© Richmond Publishing, S.A. de C.V. 2014
Av. Río Mixcoac No. 274, Col. Acacias,
Del. Benito Juárez, C.P. 03240, Ciudad de México

Publisher: Justine Piekarowicz
Editorial Team: Griselda Cacho, Rodrigo Caudillo, Diane Hermanson
Art and Design Coordinator: Marisela Pérez
Pre-Press Coordinator: Daniel Santillán

Illustrations: Sonia Alins, *Beehive Illustration*: Jim Peacock

Photographs: C. Contreras; GARCÍA-PELAYO/Juancho; J. Jaime; Prats i Camps; S. Enríquez; S. Padura; TERRANOVA INTERPRETACIÓN Y GESTION AMBIENTAL; A. G. E. FOTOSTOCK/Zhuoming Liang, Gary Meszaros, ARCO/C Hütter, Peter Jobst, JGI; GETTY IMAGES SALES SPAIN/Photos.com Plus; HIGHRES PRESS STOCK/AbleStock.com; I. PREYSLER; ISTOCKPHOTO; JOHN FOXX IMAGES; NASA/NASA Headquarters - Greatest Images of NASA (NASA-HQ-GRIN); PHOTODISC; SEIS X SEIS; MATTON-BILD; SERIDEC PHOTOIMAGENES CD/ Image Source Limited; ARCHIVO SANTILLANA

Cover Design: Leandro Pauloni

Cover Photograph: THINKSTOCK; iStockphoto

All rights reserved. No part of this work may be reproduced, stored in a retrieval system or transmitted in any form or by any means without prior written permission from the Publisher.

Richmond publications may contain links to third party websites or apps. We have no control over the content of these websites or apps, which may change frequently, and we are not responsible for the content or the way it may be used with our materials. Teachers and students are advised to exercise discretion when accessing the links.

The Publisher has made every effort to trace the owner of copyright material; however, the Publisher will correct any involuntary omission at the earliest opportunity.

First published by Richmond Publishing / Santillana Educación S.L.

Printed in China

Contents

0 Welcome back!......2
1 Time for School!......5
2 Where are you from?......13
3 Months......21
Review 1......29

4 My Town......33
5 Let's eat!......41
6 Minibeasts......49
Review 2......57

7 Space......61
8 Summer Camp......69
Review 3......77

Welcome back!

LESSON 1

1 Listen and sing.

Here we are in school again,
It's great to be with all my friends.
Hello, hello and how are you?
I'm very well, thanks! How about you?

Lots of fantastic things to do,
Reading, writing, playing too.
Lots of fantastic things to see,
I have all my friends with me.

2 Read and listen. Ask a friend.

LESSON 2

3 Listen and repeat the chant.

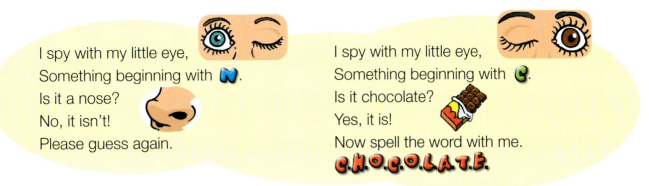

I spy with my little eye,
Something beginning with N.
Is it a nose?
No, it isn't!
Please guess again.

I spy with my little eye,
Something beginning with C.
Is it chocolate?
Yes, it is!
Now spell the word with me.
C-H-O-C-O-L-A-T-E.

4 Look and spell.

LESSON 3

5 Listen and read.

6 Play a game in pairs.

1. Time for School!

LESSON 1

1 Listen and sing.

Hurry up! It's time for school!
Time for school, time for school!
Hurry up! It's time for school!
Don't be late!
School is cool!

We love music and PE,
Spanish, art and IT!

Science, math and English too!
So many things to learn and do!

2 Ask a friend.

math   Spanish   PE   music

science   IT   art   English

LESSON 2

3 Listen and read.

 Hello, Dan, **what do you have today?**

 It's Monday. **I have science and PE.**

 Do you have music?

 No, I don't. I have music on Friday.

 Me too!

 What do you have today, Olga?

 I have English and IT.

 Do you have math?

 Yes, at nine o'clock.

 Look! It's nine o'clock now!

 Oh yes! Bye, Dan!

 Good-bye, Olga!

4 Make a class schedule and ask a friend.

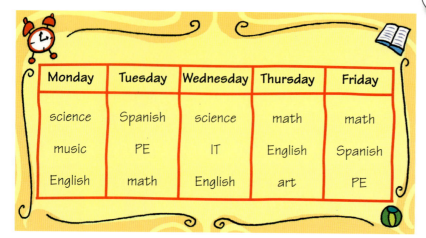

Monday	Tuesday	Wednesday	Thursday	Friday
science	Spanish	science	math	math
music	PE	IT	English	Spanish
English	math	English	art	PE

What do you have today? It's Thursday!

I have math, English and art.

LESSON 3

5 Listen and say the schoolbag.

6 Read and say *True* or *False*.

My Favorite Day

Hi! My name's Alice.
My favorite day is Thursday.
  In the morning, I have IT and music. IT is my favorite subject. I like playing games and writing stories on the computer. In music class, I like playing the guitar.
  In the afternoon, I have science. I like studying plants in science class.
  After school on Thursdays, I go to swimming club with my friends. It's a fantastic day!

1 Alice's favorite day is Tuesday.
2 Her favorite subject is IT.
3 She has music in the afternoon.
4 She doesn't like playing the guitar.
5 She likes studying plants.
6 After school, she goes to tennis club.

Late for School!

LESSON 4

7 Read and listen to the story.

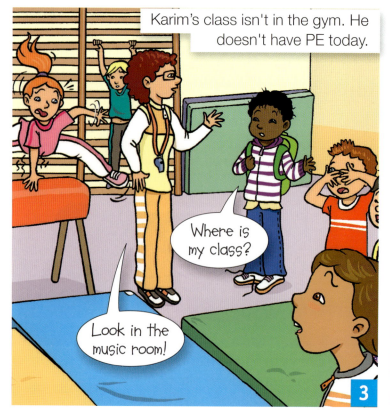

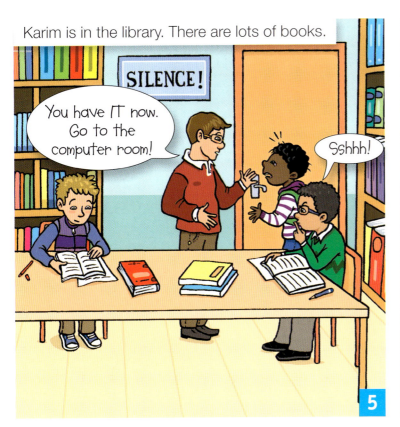

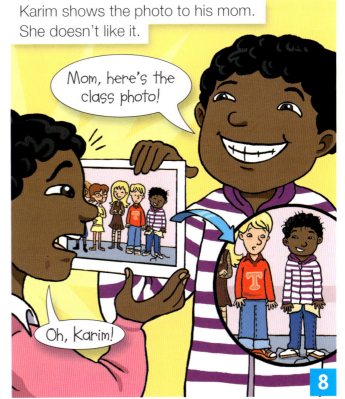

LESSON 5

8 Listen and repeat.

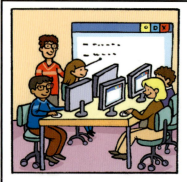
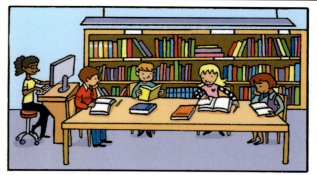
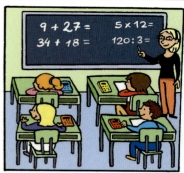

Here's our classroom. Can you see?
We're learning math, my friends and me.

In the gym we jump and climb.
We all have a fantastic time!

In the library, there are books.
Come with me and take a look!

The cafeteria is where we meet,
When it's time for us to eat.

My favorite subject is IT,
The computer room's the place for me!

We go to the playground every day,
To see our friends and run and play!

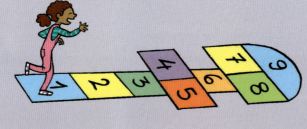

9 Say and guess.

You can't run or jump here. You can read books. Where am I?

You're in the library!

CLIL

LESSON 6

10 Read and match.

Hello, I'm Kate. Look at the photos of the playground at my school.

1

A We have a games area. You can run and jump here.

B This is the quiet area. We read books and talk with our friends here.

2

D We have a sports area. You can play basketball, soccer and table tennis here.

3

C This is our jungle gym. Climbing's difficult for me, but I like it.

4

11 Design a playground.

Beep's World!

LITERACY

LESSON 7

12 Read and listen.

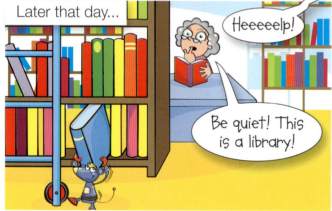

13 Listen and say a tongue twister.

2. Where are you from?

LESSON 1

1 Listen and sing.

Do you know the countries rap?
Sing along with me!
Can you find them on the map?
How many countries can you see?

Ireland, France and the UK,
And over here, is the USA.
Can you point to Mexico?

How many countries do you know?
China, Italy and Spain,
Let's sing the countries rap again!

2 Ask a friend.

Mexico   Spain   Ireland   France

USA   Italy   China   UK

How do you spell **Mexico**?

M-E-X-I-C-O

LESSON 2

3 Listen and read.

 Hi, my name's Karim.

 Hello, I'm Tania.

 Where are you from?

 I'm from Italy.

 Do you like skateboarding?

 Yes, it's my favorite sport.

 Look! He's skateboarding with his hands.

 That's Mickey Moon. He's fantastic!

 Where's he from?

 He's from the USA.

 And look at that girl. She's jumping!

 Yes, that's Rosie Ryan. She's from Ireland.

 She's great!

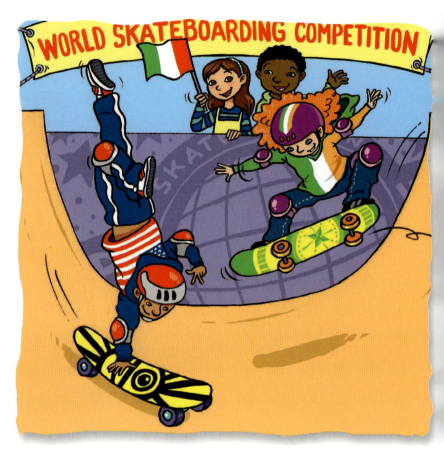

4 Ask and answer in pairs.

LESSON 3

5 Listen and read. Then listen and say *True* or *False*.

My name's Nico. I'm from Italy. I speak Italian and English.

I'm Marta. I'm from Spain. I speak Spanish and English.

My name's Jia. I'm from China. I speak Chinese, English and Spanish.

I'm Ahmed. I'm from France. I speak French, English and Arabic.

6 Read the e-mails and write about you.

Hello friends!
My name's Sam. I'm nine years old.
I'm from the USA. I speak English, Spanish and French.
My hobbies are swimming and playing the guitar.
Please write to me!

Hi!
My name's Alicia. I'm eight years old. I'm from Mexico. I speak English, Spanish and Italian.
My hobbies are listening to music and writing to my key pals!
Please write to me!

15

The Concert!

LESSON 4

7 Read and listen to the story.

Lucy likes listening to music and dancing. Her favorite singer is Sheena Shine. Sheena is from Mexico and she's very smart. She can speak Spanish, English and French.

1

Tom doesn't like Sheena Shine.

2

Everybody likes Sheena Shine. There are no tickets left.

3

Lucy is very sad. She wants to go to the concert.

4

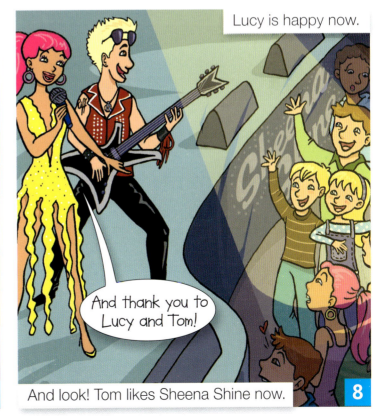

LESSON 5

8 Read and match.

1

2

Paul is from France.
He likes painting,
And swimming in the sea.

Flor likes skiing,
And singing songs.
She's from Italy.

Ling is from China.
She likes cycling,
And reading comics too!

Marc likes dancing.
He's from Spain.
What about you?

3

4

9 Read and identify the picture.

1 Tara is from Ireland.
She likes listening to music.

2 Roberto is from Mexico.
He likes playing basketball.

3 Lorna is from the UK.
She likes taking photos.

4 Mac is from the USA.
He likes surfing.

A
B
C
D

CLIL

LESSON 6

10 Read about China and Brazil.

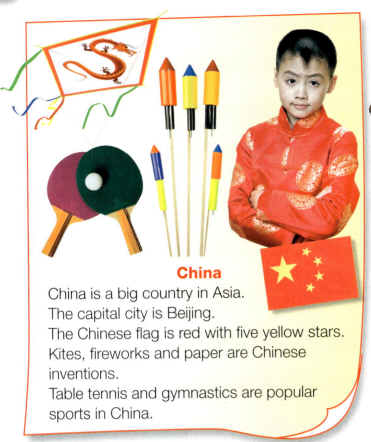

China
China is a big country in Asia.
The capital city is Beijing.
The Chinese flag is red with five yellow stars.
Kites, fireworks and paper are Chinese inventions.
Table tennis and gymnastics are popular sports in China.

Brazil
Brazil is a big country too. It's in South America. Brasilia is the capital city.
The Brazilian flag is green, blue and yellow.
You can visit the Amazon rain forest in Brazil.
Jaguars and parrots live there.
Soccer and volleyball are popular sports in Brazil.

11 Read and identify the country.

1. The flag is green, blue and yellow.
2. Gymnastics is a popular sport there.
3. You can see jaguars there.
4. It's a big country in Asia.

12 Take the quiz. Listen and check your answers. 2.5

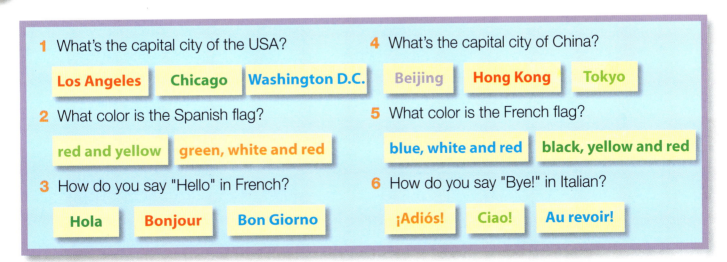

1. What's the capital city of the USA?
   Los Angeles | Chicago | Washington D.C.
2. What color is the Spanish flag?
   red and yellow | green, white and red
3. How do you say "Hello" in French?
   Hola | Bonjour | Bon Giorno
4. What's the capital city of China?
   Beijing | Hong Kong | Tokyo
5. What color is the French flag?
   blue, white and red | black, yellow and red
6. How do you say "Bye!" in Italian?
   ¡Adiós! | Ciao! | Au revoir!

Beep's World!

LITERACY

LESSON 7

13 Read and listen.

14 Listen and say a tongue twister.

Jake and Jane on their way,
Take a plane to the USA!

3. Months

LESSON 1

1 Read and say.

January, February, March,
The first three months of the year.

April, May, June, July,
Sunny days are here.

August and September,
Back to school with books and pens.

October, November, December,
Another year begins again.

2 Ask your friends.

21

LESSON 2

3 Listen and read.

Olga's cousin is visiting for Christmas. His name's Ricky and he's from Australia.

 Hi, Ricky! Do you like Christmas?

 Yes, I do. But in Australia it's hot and sunny on Christmas.

 Oh yes? **What do you wear?**

 I wear shorts and a T-shirt.

 Oh! I wear a sweater on Christmas. What do you eat?

 My family has a big barbecue. I eat hot dogs and salad.

 Oh! I don't eat salad on Christmas. I eat turkey, vegetables and potatoes. **Where do you go?**

 I go to the beach with my family. I swim in the ocean.

 Fantastic! I want to go to Australia for Christmas!

4 Ask a friend.

1 What do you wear in January?
2 What do you wear in July?
3 Where do you go in August?
4 Where do you go in December?
5 What do you eat on Christmas?
6 What do you eat in June?

LESSON 3

5 Listen and name the month.

1 February   2 July   3 October   4 December

6 Look and say in pairs.

"In January, I don't wear a T-shirt."

"In January, I wear a T-shirt in the gym."

The Snow Monster!

LESSON 4

7 Read and listen to the story.

1

2

3

4

Find and say!

5

Tom is trying to scare Ricky. 6

Now, Tom is scared! 7

8

LESSON 5

8 Listen and sing.

Seasons come, seasons go,
Some bring rain and some bring snow.
Some bring wind and some bring sun.
Which is your favorite one?

In the spring, there's lots of rain.
All the flowers come out again.
In the summer, there's no school.
We go swimming in the pool!

In autumn, all the leaves fall down,
Red and yellow, orange and brown.
In winter, when the cold winds blow,
We go skiing in the snow!

9 Read about Tessa and Max. Look and say.

Hello! I'm Tessa.
My favorite season is spring.
I like flowers and baby animals.
I wear a jacket and pants.
I ride my bike in the park.
I eat chocolate eggs at Easter.

Hi! I'm Max.
My favorite season is autumn.
I like the red and yellow leaves.
I wear a hat and a coat.
I play soccer with my friends.
I eat grapes and apples.

1   2  3  4  5  6

CLIL

LESSON 6

10 Read. Then listen and answer *True* or *False*.

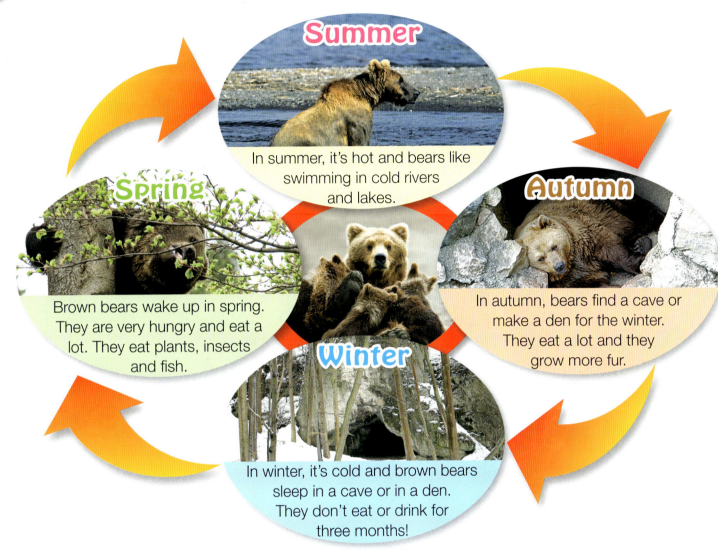

Summer

In summer, it's hot and bears like swimming in cold rivers and lakes.

Spring

Brown bears wake up in spring. They are very hungry and eat a lot. They eat plants, insects and fish.

Autumn

In autumn, bears find a cave or make a den for the winter. They eat a lot and they grow more fur.

Winter

In winter, it's cold and brown bears sleep in a cave or in a den. They don't eat or drink for three months!

11 Read the incredible facts.

Do you know?

1

Brown bears live in Spain, the USA, Russia and other countries. In Spain, they are an endangered species.

2

Brown bears stand on two legs to find food. They are two meters tall!

3

Brown bears like to eat honey!

Beep's World!

LITERACY

LESSON 7

12 Read and listen.

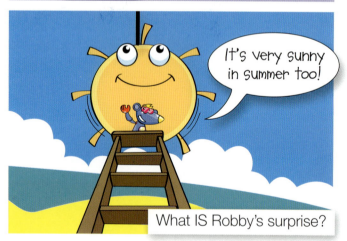
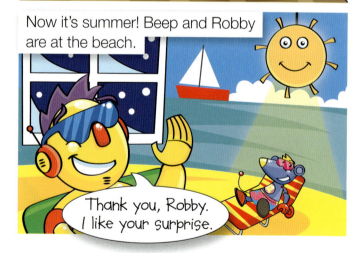

13 Listen and say a tongue twister.

November, December,
Remember, remember.
When you get dressed,
Wear a vest!

Review 1

1. When's your birthday?
2. Name it!
3. spring summer ... ...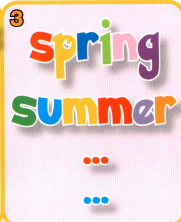
4. Do you have science on Tuesday?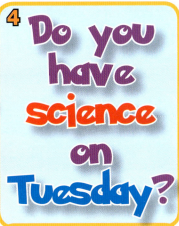
5. Where's he from?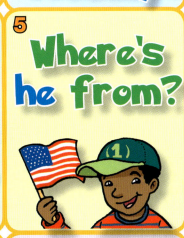
6. Where do you go in August?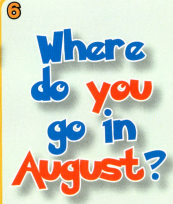
7. Where is she?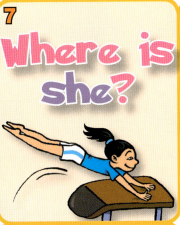
8. What do you have on Friday?
9. What's your favorite school subject?
10. March April ... ...
11. Where are you from?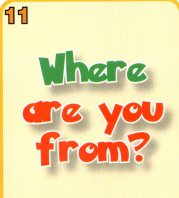
12. Name it!
13. Where's he from?
14. What do you wear in January?
15. Where's she from?
16. July August ... ...

29

1 Ask a friend.

1. What do you have on Wednesday?
2. Do you like PE?
3. Do you have English on Monday?
4. What do you have on Thursday?
5. Do you have art on Tuesday?
6. Do you like music?

2 Describe and ask a question.

3 Read and write in your notebook about your favorite month.

Hi, my name's David.
My favorite month is August. I go back to school and I see my friends again. It's hot and I wear a T-shirt and shorts.
After school, I do homework and I play computer games.
My birthday is in August. I have a party with my family.

4. My Town

LESSON 1

1 Listen and sing.

My town, my town,
It's a wonderful place to be!

In my town, there's lots to see.
A shopping mall and a library,
There's a museum and a
movie theater too.
There's a park and a hospital
and a zoo!

There's a train station
and a swimming pool.
I think my town is really cool,
So many things to see and do.
It's home for me and it's home for you!

2 Listen and say the place.

shopping mall

museum

movie theater

park

hospital

zoo

swimming pool

train station

33

LESSON 2

3 Listen and read.

 Hello, Karim. **Is there a swimming pool in your town?**

 Yes, there is. Do you like swimming?

 Yes, it's my favorite sport. Is there a zoo?

 No, there isn't, but there's a big park.

 Is there a museum?

 Yes, there is.

 Is there a movie theater?

 Yes, there is. Do you like movies?

 Yes, I like superhero movies.

 Me too! Let's go to the movies later!

4 Look at the picture for one minute. Cover, then ask and answer in pairs.

LESSON 3

5 Listen and say the town. Then listen and check. 4.4

6 Read and say *True* or *False*.

1 There isn't a library in Green Town.
2 There's a hospital in Yellow Town.
3 There's a movie theater in Blue Town.
4 There isn't a zoo in Green Town.
5 There's a train station in Yellow Town and Green Town.
6 There isn't a swimming pool in Green Town.

7 Read and ask.

35

The Science Museum!

LESSON 4

8 Read and listen to the story.

Dad is reading a newspaper. Lucy and Tom don't want to watch TV.

Dad likes museums. They are going to the science museum. Tom calls Karim and Olga.

Karim has his camera. He's taking a photo.

Oh no! Olga is scared of spiders. But Lucy likes the robots. **5**

The magnets help Lucy fly. **6**

7

Lucy has a new T-shirt. She thinks museums are fun now! **8**

LESSON 5

9 Read and number.

1 What should we do today?
Tell me, what should we do?
Let's go to the science museum!
You can come too!

2 What should we do today?
Tell me, what should we do?
Let's go to the swimming pool!
You can come too!

3 What should we do today?
Tell me, what should we do?
Let's go to the shopping mall!
You can come too!

10 Look and read. Make plans with a friend.

38

CLIL

LESSON 6

1 Read and match.

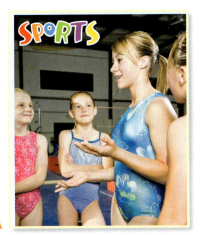

A

B

Hi! I'm Anita. This is my town.

1. In my town, there's a bus station and a train station. When it's raining, I go to school by bus. When it's sunny, I walk to school.

2. There's a sports center and a swimming pool. My favorite sport is gymnastics. I do gymnastics with my friends at the sports center.

C

D

3. In June, there's a kite festival in my town. I don't have a kite, but I like taking photos of the kites.

4. My favorite place is the park. I go to the park with my mom and dad on Sundays. We ride our bikes and have a picnic.

12 Listen and say *True* or *False*. 4.6

13 Write about where you live.

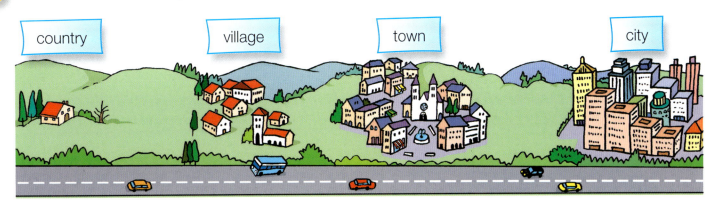

country　　village　　town　　city

39

Beep's World!

LITERACY

LESSON 7

14 Read and listen.

15 Listen and say a tongue twister.

Luke and Sue
go to the zoo,
after school.
You can come too!
It's cool!

5. Let's eat!

LESSON 1

1 Listen and sing.

Are you hungry?
Let's all eat!
Come to the table and take a seat.

For breakfast there's cereal, eggs and ham.
And lots of toast with strawberry jam.

For lunch there's vegetables, burgers and rice.
All this food is very nice.

Soup and salad, fish and meat.
So many tasty things to eat!

2 Look and tell.

What are your favorite kinds of food?

Ham, soup and salad.

eggs | ham | cereal | burger | salad

meat | rice | vegetables | soup | toast

LESSON 2

3 Listen and read. 5.2

 Are you hungry?

 Yes, I am.

 Me too! Let's eat!

 How much is the soup?

 It's four dollars and fifty cents.

 How much is the salad?

 It's three dollars and seventy-five cents.

 How much is the ham sandwich?

 It's two dollars and ninety cents.

 Perfect! I have two dollars and ninety cents!

 And I have five dollars. OK, the ham sandwich for you and the soup for me!

4 Play the game and ask a friend.

LESSON 3

5 Read about Karim's meals.

breakfast

I have breakfast at eight o'clock. I have cereal, milk and a banana for breakfast. I like reading comics in the morning.

lunch

I have lunch at one thirty. I talk to my friends at lunch. I have meat, vegetables and yogurt for lunch.

dinner

I have dinner at seven o'clock. I have soup and toast for dinner. I tell my sister stories.

6 Complete the chart.

	time	food
breakfast	eight o'clock	cereal, milk, banana
lunch		
dinner		

7 Ask a friend.

1. What do you have for breakfast?
2. What do you have for lunch?
3. What do you have for dinner?

The School Fair!

LESSON 4

8 Read and listen to the story.

The principal likes Tom's unusual sandwiches.

Egon Ronald likes the fish and jam sandwich!

LESSON 5

9 Read and chant.

Can I have an apple?
Can I have a cake?
Can I have a sandwich?
And a big milkshake?

Can I have a pizza,
With ham and cheese?
And can I have an ice cream?
Please! Please! Please!

10 Look, read and say the price. Play with a friend.

Can I have an egg sandwich and water, please?

Yes, that's two dollars and seventy cents.

Can I have a cheese sandwich and a milkshake, please?

Can I have a ham sandwich and a juice, please?

Can I have a chicken sandwich and a bottle of water, please?

CLIL

LESSON 6

1 Read and label.

Fruit and vegetables **Fats and sugars** **Proteins** **Carbohydrates**

Chocolate, candy, soft drinks and cake have a lot of sugar. Eat a little.

Cheese, milk, meat and fish contain proteins. Proteins help children grow and be strong. Eat two or three servings a day.

Fruit and vegetables come from plants. Eat four or five servings a day.

Pasta, rice, bread and potatoes contain carbohydrates. Carbohydrates give us energy. Eat five or six servings a day.

12 Listen and answer *True* or *False*. Then listen and check. 5.4

Beep's World!

LITERACY

LESSON 7

13 Read and listen.

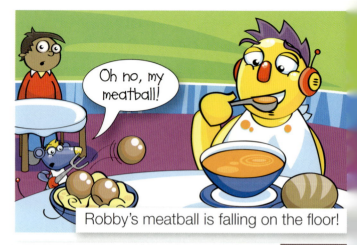

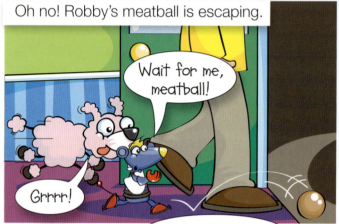

14 Listen and say a tongue twister.

Can I have a sandwich,
with salad and ham,
and carrot and apple,
and strawberry jam?

6. Minibeasts

LESSON 1

1 Listen and sing.

Minibeasts are everywhere,
Look behind you!
Don't be scared!
In the garden, take a look.
Read about them in a book.

Dragonflies and ladybugs,
Living in the trees.
Grasshoppers and wriggly worms,
Butterflies and bees.

Ants and snails and centipedes,
Crawling through the grass.
Look and you can see them,
With your magnifying glass.

2 Describe and guess in pairs.

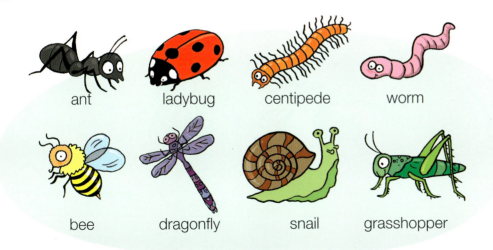

ant   ladybug   centipede   worm

bee   dragonfly   snail   grasshopper

It's pink. It can't fly.

The worm!

one dragon**fly**

two dragon**flies**!

49

LESSON 2

3 Read about bees. Listen and answer *True* or *False*.

Bees are insects. They are yellow and black. They live in big colonies.

1. They have four wings. They can fly.
2. They have two eyes and a mouth. They don't have ears.
3. They have six legs. They can walk.
4. They have two antennae. They can smell flowers with their antennae.
5. They have a stinger.

4 Read the questions with a friend and answer. Then listen and check.

Do snails have ears?

Do ladybugs have wings?

No, they don't.

Yes, they do.

1. Do snails have ears?
2. Do grasshoppers have antennae?
3. Do ladybugs have six legs?
4. Do centipedes have stingers?
5. Do worms have eyes?
6. Do ants have antennae?

- 5 or 6 correct answers: Fantastic! You're a minibeast expert.
- 3 or 4 correct answers: You are good at science.
- 1 or 2 correct answers: Oh no! Go to the park and look at minibeasts today!

LESSON 3

5 Listen and read.

 Do you like grasshoppers, Olga?

 Yes, they're my favorite minibeasts!

 How many legs do they have?

 They have six legs. They can jump and walk.

 How many wings do they have?

 They have four wings. They can fly.

 How many antennae do they have?

 They have two antennae.

 How many eyes do they have?

 They have two big eyes. Are grasshoppers your favorite minibeasts too?

 No, my favorite minibeasts are butterflies!

6 Read and identify the minibeast.

snail ladybug ant centipede

1 They have six legs and two small antennae. Only queens and males have wings.
2 They don't have wings or legs. They have a big shell.
3 They don't have wings. They have two eyes and thirty legs.
4 They have two wings and six legs. They have two small antennae.

The Giant Australian Treefly!

LESSON 4

7 Read and listen to the story.

1

2

3

4

LESSON 5

8 Read and label.

The garden is my favorite place,
I like to smell the **flowers**,
And watch the little minibeasts,
For hours and hours and hours.

There's a ladybug behind a **leaf**,
And spiders in the **trees**.
Frogs and goldfish in the **pond**,
And lots of ants and bees.

I like to sit down on the **grass**
And look up at the sky.
I listen to the buzzing bees,
And watch the clouds go by.

9 Look and ask a friend.

Where's the fish?

Where's the snail?

It's in the pond.

It's behind the leaf.

CLIL

LESSON 6

10 Read about carnivores, herbivores and omnivores.

- Crocodiles, lions and dragonflies are carnivores. They eat other animals.
- Elephants, rabbits and caterpillars are herbivores. They eat plants, fruit and flowers.
- Squirrels, ants and ladybugs are omnivores. They eat other animals and plants.

11 Look and read.

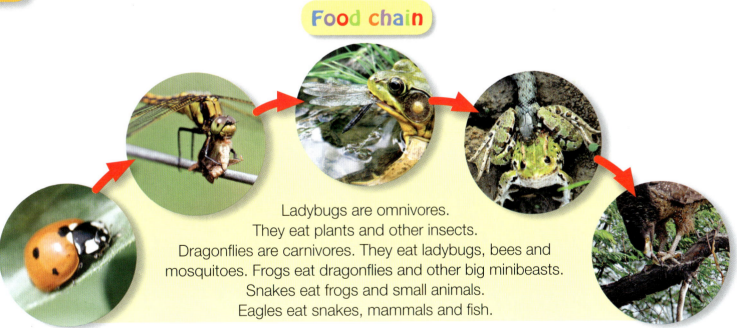

Food chain

Ladybugs are omnivores.
They eat plants and other insects.
Dragonflies are carnivores. They eat ladybugs, bees and mosquitoes. Frogs eat dragonflies and other big minibeasts.
Snakes eat frogs and small animals.
Eagles eat snakes, mammals and fish.

12 Read and say *True* or *False*.

1. Omnivores eat animals and plants.
2. Rabbits are herbivores.
3. Dragonflies eat plants.
4. Snakes eat frogs and small animals.

Beep's World!

LITERACY

LESSON 7

13 Read and listen.

14 Listen and say a tongue twister.

John and Ron near the pond,
Sitting on a log.
Don't put on your sock, John.
Look! There's a frog!

Review 2

1 Name and spell!

2 Is there a movie theater in your town?

3 How much is the soup?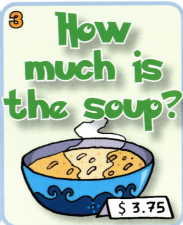
$ 3.75

4 What do you have for breakfast?

8 They have ... They don't have ...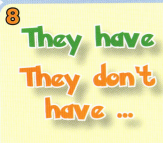

7 Is there a museum in your town?

6 Name and spell!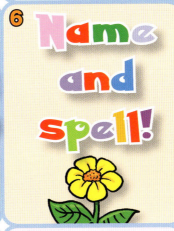

5 Name five minibeasts.

9 How much is the burger?
$ 2.35

10 What do you have for dinner?

11 Where's the bee?

12 In my town, there's a...

16 Name and spell!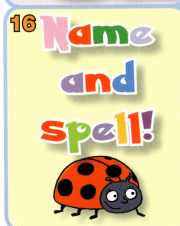

15 How many legs do spiders have?

14 Name!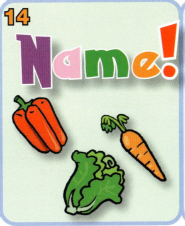

13 Name six foods.

1 Read and say *True* or *False*.

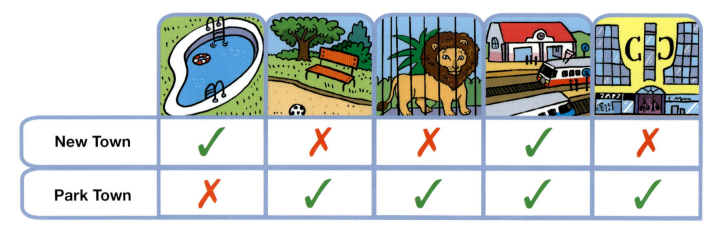

1. There isn't a swimming pool in Park Town.
2. There's a train station in New Town.
3. There's a park in New Town and Park Town.
4. There isn't a shopping mall in Park Town.
5. There's a zoo in New Town and Park Town.
6. There's a swimming pool in New Town.

2 Look and calculate. Then ask a friend.

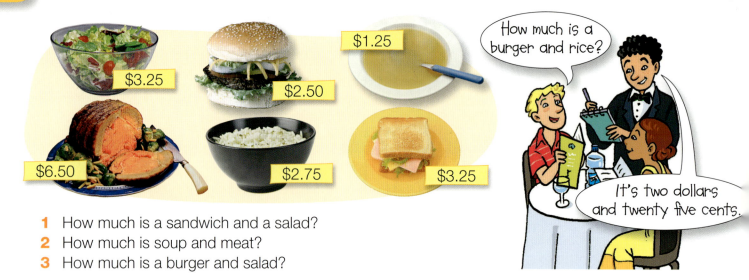

1. How much is a sandwich and a salad?
2. How much is soup and meat?
3. How much is a burger and salad?

3 Read and identify. Describe and guess with a friend.

7. Space

LESSON 1

1 Listen and sing.

I want to be an astronaut,
Flying to the stars.
And travel in my spaceship,
To Jupiter and Mars.

I look up through my telescope,
At comets zooming by,
And satellites and UFOs,
Above us in the sky.

I want to see the planets,
The stars, the Moon and Sun.
It's great to be an astronaut,
It's such fantastic fun!

2 Ask in pairs.

How do you spell **planet**?

P–L–A–N–E–T

star   telescope   comet   Moon

spaceship   planet   UFO   satellite

61

LESSON 2

3 Listen and read. 7.2

 Hi, Olga! Who's this?

 This is Emma Castro. She's a famous astronaut.

 Does she work on a space station?

 Yes, she does. She takes photos of space and she does experiments.

 What does she eat?

 She eats cereal, soup and sandwiches. She doesn't eat salad; there aren't any fresh vegetables on a space station!

 Does she wear a spacesuit on the space station?

 No, she doesn't. She wears T-shirts and pants.

 Does she sleep in a bed?

 No, she doesn't. She sleeps in a special sleeping bag.

 Do you want to be an astronaut?

Yes, I do! I want to go to the Moon!

4 Look at Emma Castro's schedule. Ask and answer.

6:00	get up
6:30	ride the exercise bike
7:00	take a shower
7:30	have breakfast
8:00	take photos
9:30	write e-mails
10:30	do experiments
12:00	have lunch

Hi! I'm Emma. I'm an astronaut. I live on a space station and this is my schedule. I ride an exercise bike every morning.

Does she have breakfast at seven o'clock?   ✗ No, she doesn't.
Does she write e-mails at nine thirty?   ✓ Yes, she does.

62

LESSON 3

5 Read and number the pictures.

Free time on a space station

1 What does an astronaut do in the evening?
This is Robert Green. He's an astronaut from the USA and he lives on a space station. In the evening, he doesn't work. He reads books and listens to music.

2 What does an astronaut do on Sundays?
Robert doesn't work on Sundays. He plays cards with the other astronauts. He writes e-mails to his family and he watches DVDs. He doesn't watch TV. There isn't a TV on a space station.

3 What does an astronaut do on Christmas Day?
Robert has dinner with the other astronauts. He sings songs and plays the guitar. He talks to his family on a special phone and says "Merry Christmas!"

4 What does an astronaut do at night?
Robert sleeps at night! He has a very special bed. It's not on the floor. It's on the wall and it has a zipper. Why does Robert have a special bed? Because there's no gravity in space!

6 Listen and say *True* or *False*. 7.3

The UFO!

LESSON 4

7 Read and listen to the story.

Aunt Stella is visiting. She lives in the USA and she works at the Space Center. She has a present for Tom and Lucy. It's a telescope. Tom likes astronomy.

1

Karim and Olga are staying with Tom and Lucy. Mom and Dad are going to a party tonight.

2

Olga is looking through the telescope.

3

4

Find and say!

Lucy is scared of the alien.

Mom and Dad are going to a costume party!

LESSON 5

8 Listen and repeat the chant.

Mercury and **Venus**,
The planets go around the **Sun**,
Earth and **Mars**,
Can you name every one?

Jupiter and **Saturn**,
Eight planets big and small,
Uranus and **Neptune**,
We can name them all!

9 Read about the planets and say *True* or *False*.

Mercury is very small. It's made of rock. It's near the Sun and is very hot. It doesn't have any moons.

Mars is called the Red Planet. It has two small moons. There are lots of mountains there and it's cold.

Saturn is very big. It's made of gas and is very cold. It has lots of rings. They're made of ice and rock. It has 52 moons.

1 There are mountains on Mars.
2 Saturn has 62 moons.
3 Mercury is made of ice.
4 Saturn's rings are made of rock and ice.
5 Mars doesn't have any moons.
6 Saturn is made of gas.

CLIL

LESSON 6

10 Look and read.

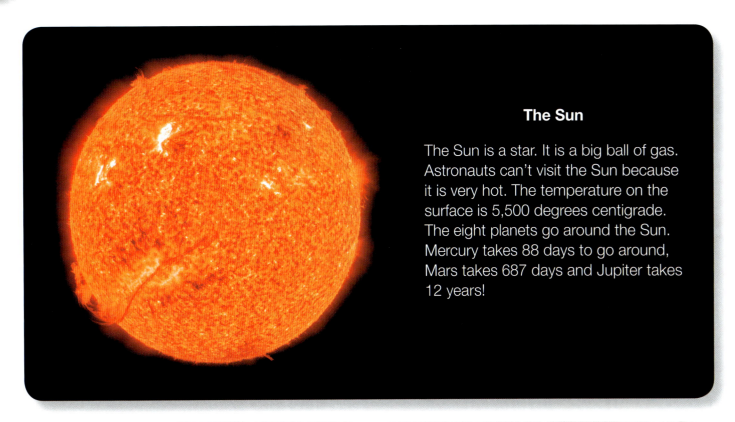

The Sun

The Sun is a star. It is a big ball of gas. Astronauts can't visit the Sun because it is very hot. The temperature on the surface is 5,500 degrees centigrade. The eight planets go around the Sun. Mercury takes 88 days to go around, Mars takes 687 days and Jupiter takes 12 years!

The Earth

The Earth is a planet. It is called the Blue Planet because 70% of the surface is water. Animals and plants can live on the Earth because there are water and air. It goes around the Sun in 365 days.

The Moon

The Moon is ¼ the size of the Earth. There isn't any air on the Moon. Animals and plants can't live there. There is ice on the Moon. It goes around the Earth in 28 days.

11 Listen and write with the Sun, the Earth or the Moon in your notebook.

Beep's World!

LITERACY

LESSON 7

12 Read and listen.

13 Listen and say a tongue twister.

Nick O'Neil's my neighbor.
He's an astronaut.
Nick's flying to Neptune tonight.
Have a nice flight!

8. Summer Camp

LESSON 1

1 Listen and sing.

When it's hot and the sky is blue,
And summer's here again,
It's time to go to summer camp,
To be with all my friends.

I want to go canoeing,
And hiking in the woods,
And horseback riding and climbing,
I think they're really good.

We sit around the campfire,
Cook hot dogs and sing songs,
And tell each other stories,
All night long!

2 Listen and say the activity.

go canoeing

go horseback riding

cook hot dogs

go hiking

play ball games

sing songs

tell stories

go climbing

LESSON 2

3 Listen and read. 8.3

  Hi, Olga! Do you want to play ball games?

 No, I don't. My legs are tired.

 Do you want to go hiking?

 No, I don't. My feet are tired.

 Do you want to go canoeing?

 No, I don't. My arms are tired.

 Do you want to cook hot dogs?

 Yes, I do. I'm hungry!

 Fantastic! Let's eat!

 Yes, and let's tell stories too!

4 Make plans with a friend.

1 Do you want to tell stories?
2 Do you want to go climbing?
3 Do you want to sing songs?
4 Do you want to go canoeing?
5 Do you want to play ball games?
6 Do you want to go horseback riding?
7 Do you want to go hiking?

70

LESSON 3

5 Read. Then listen and say the place.

6 Read and say the place.

The Rescue!

LESSON 4

7 Read and listen to the story. 8.5

Find and say!

The children are helping to rescue the man.

Everyone is sitting around the campfire singing songs and cooking hot dogs.

LESSON 5

8 Repeat the chant and number.

We're going hiking in the woods,
So don't forget to pack,
A water bottle and a flashlight,
A raincoat and a snack.

And don't forget your compass,
And don't forget your map,
And if the weather's sunny,
Please don't forget your cap!

☐ water bottle ☐ flashlight
☐ snack ☐ cap
☐ compass ☐ map
☐ raincoat

9 Play a guessing game in pairs.

Do you have a water bottle?
No, I don't.
Do you have a compass?
Yes, I do.
You're Bill!

74

CLIL

LESSON 6

10 Look and say.

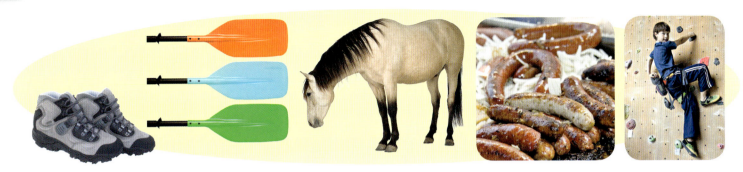

11 Read and look at the survey.

Activities	Tally Marks	Total
hiking	///	3
ball games	//// //	7
horseback riding	//	2
canoeing	//// ////	10
telling stories	////	5
climbing	////	4

12 Look at the bar chart. Listen and say *True* or *False*. 8.6

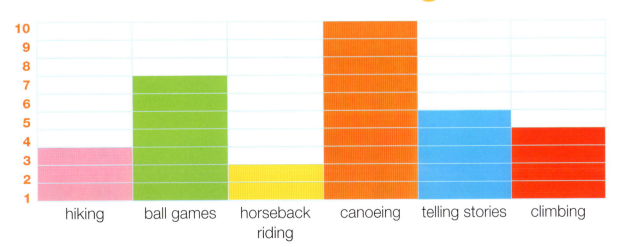

13 Do a survey and write it in your notebook.

Beep's World!

LITERACY

LESSON 7

14 Read and listen.

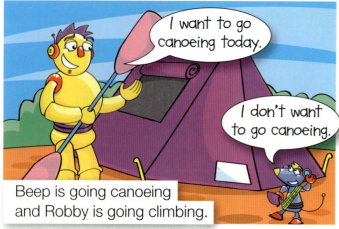

15 Listen and say a tongue twister.

Hiking, canoeing and running.
Swimming and climbing and riding my bike.
Drawing and painting and singing and playing.
These are the things that I like!

Review 3

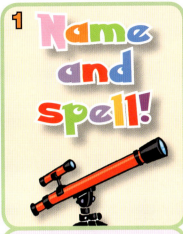
1 Name and spell!

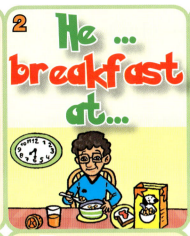
2 He ... breakfast at...

3 Do you want to go canoeing this summer?

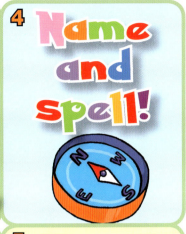
4 Name and spell!

8 Do you have a flashlight?

7 Name and spell!
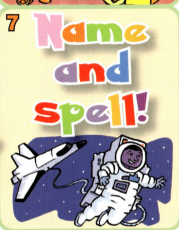

6 I want to ....
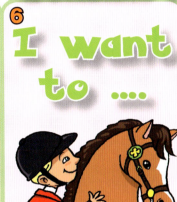

5 It's a big planet with rings. What's its name?

9 Does she have lunch at one o'clock?

10 Name five planets.
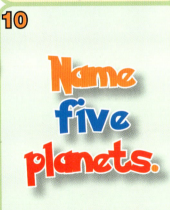

11 She ... photos at...
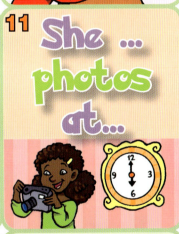

12 Do you want to go horseback riding this summer?

16 Do you want to go hiking this summer?

15 I don't want to...

14 Name and spell!
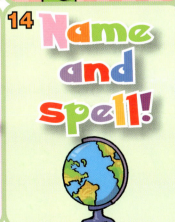

13 Name it!
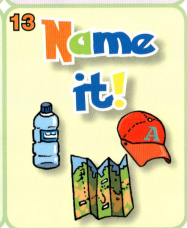

1 Copy and complete.

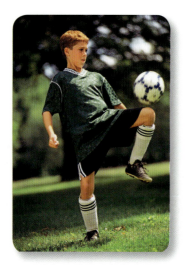

Saturday
8:30 get up
9:00 have breakfast
10:00 go to swimming club
12:00 do homework
1:30 have lunch
3:00 read books
4:00 play soccer in the park
7:00 have dinner

1 He plays soccer at…
2 He does homework at…
3 He has breakfast at…
4 He … at seven o'clock.
5 He … at one thirty.
6 He … at three o'clock.

2 Ask a friend about the summer vacation.

1 Do you want to go horseback riding?
2 Do you want to play ball games?
3 Do you want to read books?
4 Do you want to go to the beach?
5 Do you want to go camping?
6 Do you want to do homework?

3 Read and write about your summer plans.

Hi, I'm Claudia. I'm from Italy.
This summer, I want to go to the mountains with my family. I want to go canoeing and hiking. I don't want to go climbing. I don't like climbing.
At night, I want to cook hot dogs and tell stories with my cousins.
Your friend,
Claudia

Activity Book

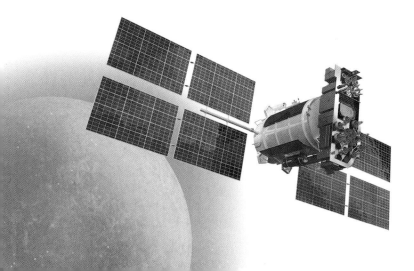

Contents

0 Welcome back!......2

1 Time for School!......3

2 Where are you from?......5

3 Months......7

4 My Town......9

5 Let's eat!......11

6 Minibeasts......13

7 Space......15

8 Summer Camp......17

Picture Dictionary......19

Beep on Grammar......27

Track List......35

Welcome back!

1 Read, look and circle.

Hi! My name's **Anna** / **Sally**.
I'm **eight** / **nine** years old.
I **like** / **don't like** reading.
My favorite sport is **gymnastics** / **tennis**.
I have a **cat** / **fish**.
Bye!

2 Write in order and answer.

1 name   your   What's
_____?   _____

2 you   old   How   are
_____?   _____

3 like   swimming   Do   you
_____?   _____

4 food   favorite   What's   your
_____?   _____

5 a   Do   pet   have   you
_____?   _____

3 Listen and complete. 0.1

This is my friend <u>Albert</u>.
He's _____. He likes playing _____. His favorite food is _____ and he has a _____!

1. Time for School!

1 Listen and match. 1.1

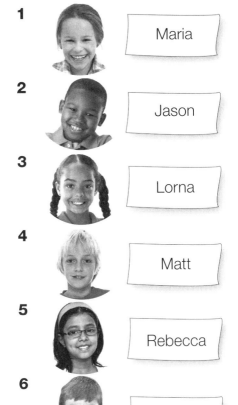

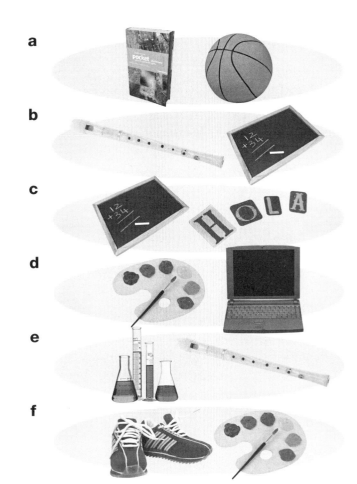

1 Maria — a
2 Jason — b
3 Lorna — c
4 Matt — d
5 Rebecca — e
6 Ben — f

2 Read and answer for you.

1 What do you have on Monday?   I have _____ and _____.
2 What do you have on Tuesday?   _____
3 What do you have on Wednesday? _____
4 What do you have on Thursday?   _____
5 What do you have on Friday?   _____

3 Make your class schedule in English in your notebook.

Time	Monday	Tuesday	Wednesday	Thursday	Friday
9:00					

Review

1 Look and write.

2 Complete the sentences.

Monday	Tuesday	Wednesday	Thursday	Friday
English	PE	science	music	Spanish
art	math	IT	English	math

1 I have PE and math on _____.
2 I have music and _____ on Thursday.
3 I have _____ and art on Monday.
4 I have science and _____ on _____.
5 I have _____ and _____ on Friday.
6 I have English on _____ and _____.

3 Read and answer for you.

1 What do you have today? _____
2 What's your favorite subject? _____
3 What's your favorite day? _____

4 Now ask two friends the questions in Activity 3.

4

2. Where are you from?

1 Listen and number. 2.1

2 Look and write.

Berta likes _____ _____.

Leonard _____ _____.

Jack _____ _____
_____ _____.

Alberta _____ _____.

5

Review

1 Look and write the names of the countries.

_____   _____   _____   _____

2 Look and complete.

English   Italian   French   Chinese   Spanish

1 I speak _____, _____ and _____.
2 I speak _____ and _____.
3 I speak _____, _____ and _____.

3 Write about the children.

playing   she   comics   skiing   he   painting   likes   soccer   reading

She likes playing basketball.   _____   _____   _____

6

3. Months

1 Listen and match.

1 January

2 February

3 June

a
b
c
d
e
f

4 May

5 October

6 November

2 Look, read and circle.

Hello, my name's Bill. In August, I **go** / **don't go** to school. I **go** / **don't go** to the beach. I **eat** / **don't eat** ice cream every day. I **wear** / **don't wear** a jacket. I **wear** / **don't wear** shorts and a T-shirt. At the beach, I **read** / **don't read** books.

3 Complete for you.

1 In July, _____ to the beach.   I **go** / **don't go**

2 In January, _____ a T-shirt.   I **wear** / **don't wear**

3 In April, _____ ice cream.   I **eat** / **don't eat**

4 In October, _____ soccer.   I **play** / **don't play**

5 In June, _____ in the sea.   I **swim** / **don't swim**

6 In August, _____ at 8 o'clock.   I **get up** / **don't get up**

7

Review

1 Circle and write in order.

DECEMBERJULYNOVEMBERMAYAPRILMARCHSEPTEMBER

January, February, _____, _____, _____, June, _____, August, _____, October, _____, _____.

2 Write *a, e, i, o, u* and match.

1 Wh__t d__ y___ __t __n s__mm__r?   a I wear a sweater.
2 Wh__r__ d__ y___ g__ __n spr__ng?   b I go to the park.
3 Wh__t d__ y___ w__ _r __n __ _t__ mn?   c I eat watermelon.

3 Look and complete.

	eat ice cream	play soccer	go to the park	wear a sweater
summer	✓	✗	✓	✗
winter	✗	✓	✓	✓

1 In summer, _____ _____ ice cream.
2 In winter, I _____ _____ sweater.
3 In _____, I don't play _____.
4 In winter, _____ _____ _____ ice cream.
5 In _____ and _____, I go to the _____.

8

4. My Town

1 Listen and check ✓ or cross ✗.

2 Write in order and circle the answers.

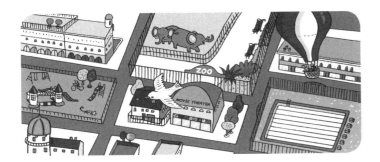

1 there mall shopping a Is

_____? Yes, there is. No, there isn't.

2 pool Is a swimming there

_____? Yes, there is. No, there isn't.

3 a there movie theater Is

_____? Yes, there is. No, there isn't.

4 park a Is there

_____? Yes, there is. No, there isn't.

3 Read and put a ✓ or a ✗ about your town.

1 There's a movie theater. ☐
2 There's a shopping mall. ☐
3 There's a museum. ☐
4 There's a park. ☐

9

Review

1 Write the questions and answer *Yes, there is* or *No, there isn't*.

Is there a _____ _____ ?
_____

Is there _____ _____ ?
_____

Is _____ _____ _____ ?
_____

_____ ?

2 Look and write suggestions.

1 Let's go to the movies!

2 _____

3 _____

4 _____

5. Let's eat!

1 Read and match.

$1.95

$4.60

$3.90

three dollars and twenty-five cents

one dollar and ninety-five cents

four dollars and seventy-five cents

three dollars and ninety cents

four dollars and sixty cents

$4.75

$3.25

2 Listen and write the prices. 5.1

3 Look at Activity 2 and complete.

1 How much is the rice?   It's _____ dollars and forty-_____ cents.
2 How much is the burger?   It's _____.
3 How much is the soup?   It's _____.

11

Review

1 Do the puzzle and find the mystery food.

2 Complete and circle the correct answer.

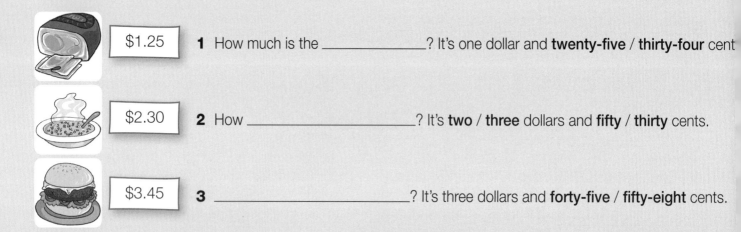

1 How much is the _____? It's one dollar and **twenty-five** / **thirty-four** cent

2 How _____? It's **two** / **three** dollars and **fifty** / **thirty** cents.

3 _____? It's three dollars and **forty-five** / **fifty-eight** cents.

3 Look and complete.

I have cereal and _____ for breakfast. I have breakfast at _____.
I have _____ at one thirty. I have ham and _____ for lunch.
I _____ dinner at _____ o'clock. I have _____ and vegetables for dinner.

6. Minibeasts

1 Listen and complete the chart. Write the name of the minibeasts. 6.1

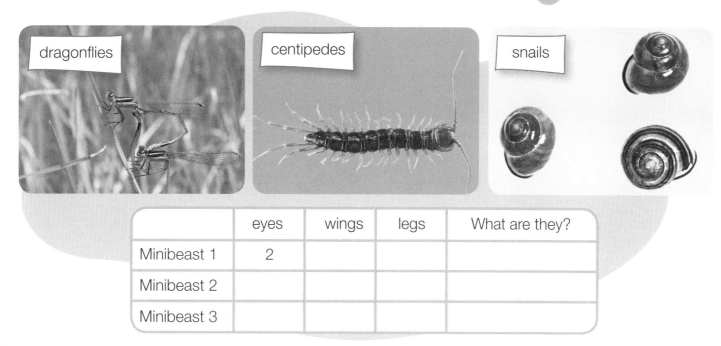

	eyes	wings	legs	What are they?
Minibeast 1	2			
Minibeast 2				
Minibeast 3				

2 Write in order and match.

1 (many) (centipedes) (do) (How) (antennae) (have)
_____? 0

2 (snails) (wings) (How) (have) (many) (do)
_____? 2

3 (do) (many) (wings) (bees) (have) (How)
_____? 6

4 (have) (grasshoppers) (legs) (How) (do) (many)
_____? 4

3 Look and write using *They have* or *They don't have*.

Spiders don't have antennae.
_____
_____
_____
_____

13

Review

1 Look and complete.

__ __ n t __ __ e __ __ __   __ __ o w __ __   __ __ a __ __   __ a __ y __ __ __ __

2 Write the questions and answer.

1 Howmanylegsdotheyhave

_____? _____

2 Dotheyhaveantennae

_____? _____

3 Howmanywingsdotheyhave

_____? _____

4 Dotheyhaveeyes

_____? _____

3 Read and complete.

    four   fruit   ears   fly   herbivores   legs

Grasshoppers

Grasshoppers are fantastic animals! They can walk, jump and _____.
They eat plants and _____. They're _____.
They have six _____. They have _____ wings.
They don't have _____, but they can hear with their bodies.

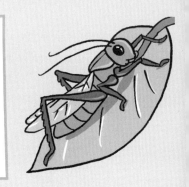

14

7. Space

1 Listen and check ✓ or cross ✗. 7.1

This is Natalia. She's an astronaut from Brazil. What does she do in the evenings?

Monday	✗	✓		✗		✓	
Tuesday							
Wednesday							
Thursday							
Friday							
Saturday							
Sunday							

2 Look at Activity 1 and complete.

doesn't play   writes   listens   doesn't write

takes   reads   plays   doesn't watch

1 Natalia _____ books on Saturday.
2 She _____ e-mails on Wednesday.
3 She _____ to music on Thursday.
4 She _____ cards on Sunday.
5 She _____ e-mails on Friday.
6 She _____ DVDs on Saturday.
7 She _____ photos on Tuesday.
8 She _____ the guitar on Friday.

15

Review

1 Look and write.

t c m e o   o n m o   p i h s p s a e c   p l n a t e   s a r t s

2 Read about Anna and circle.

Hi! I'm Anna.

On Saturday:

1 She **watches** / **doesn't watch** DVDs.
2 She **takes** / **doesn't take** photos.
3 She **reads** / **doesn't read** books.
4 She **writes** / **doesn't write** e-mails.
5 She **listens** / **doesn't listen** to music.

3 Now write about what Anna does on Sunday.

She doesn't read books.

16

8. Summer Camp

1 Listen and complete the chart. 8.1

	go hiking	sing songs	go horseback riding	go canoeing
Toby	✓	✗		
Ingrid				
Becky				
Pat				
Tina				

2 Look at Activity 1. Read and answer.

At summer camp, I don't want to go horseback riding or sing songs. I want to go hiking in the mountains and I want to go canoeing.

Who am I? _____

I like animals and I want to go horseback riding. I don't want to sing songs or go canoeing. I like mountains and I want to go hiking.

Who am I? _____

3 Look and complete.

1  2   3   4  5

1 I want to _____.
2 I don't want to _____.
3 _____
4 _____
5 _____

17

Review

1 Look and write.

_____   _____   _____   _____

2 Look and write with sentences from the chart.

| I want
I don't want | to | go climbing.
sing songs. | tell stories.
go canoeing. |

1  2  3  4

_____   _____   _____   _____
_____   _____   _____   _____

3 Complete and answer *Yes, I do* or *No, I don't.*

1 Do you want to pl__y b__ll g__m__s? _____
2 Do you want to g__ h__rs__b__ __k r__d__ng? _____
3 Do you want to c__ __k h__t d__gs? _____

18

Picture Dictionary 1

art

English

IT

math

music

PE

science

Spanish

cafeteria

classroom

computer room

gym

library

playground

19

Picture Dictionary 2

China

Mexico

France

Spain

Ireland

UK

Italy

USA

Picture Dictionary 3

January

February

March

April

May

June

July

August

September

October

November

December

spring

summer

autumn

winter

21

Picture Dictionary 4

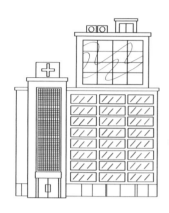 hospital

 shopping mall

 movie theater

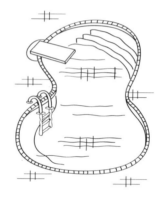 swimming pool

 museum

 train station

 park

 zoo

Picture Dictionary 5

 burger

 rice

 cereal

 salad

 eggs

 soup

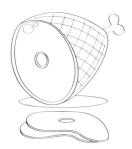 ham

 toast

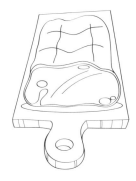 meat

 vegetables

Picture Dictionary 6

ant

bee

centipede

dragonfly

grasshopper

ladybug

snail

worm

flower

grass

leaf

pond

tree

Picture Dictionary 7

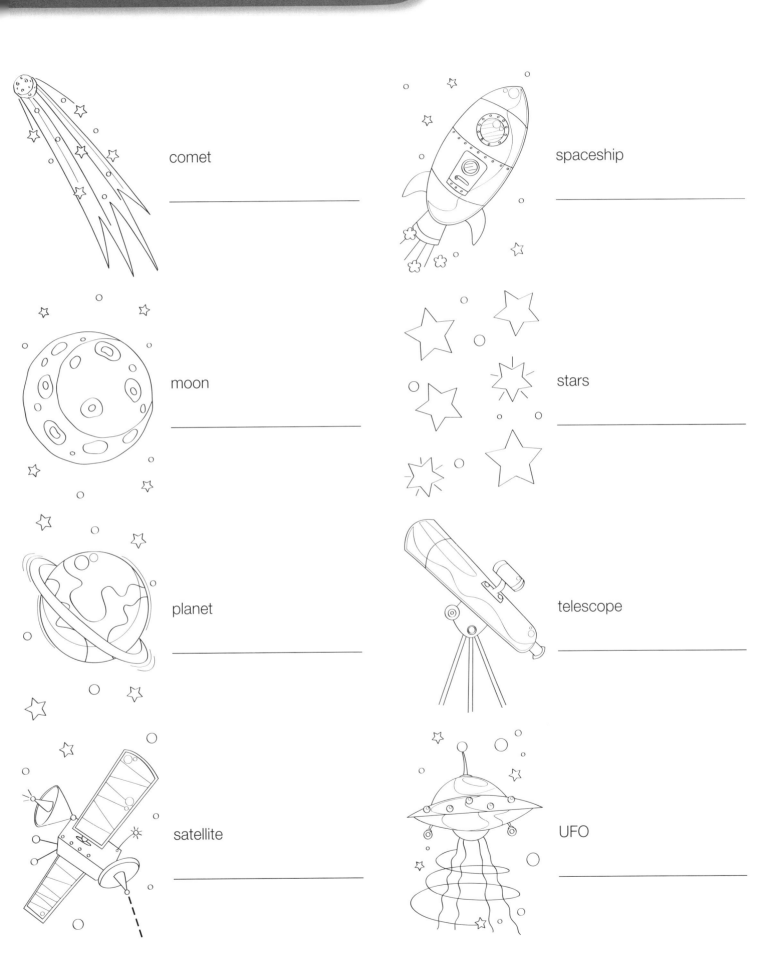

comet

spaceship

moon

stars

planet

telescope

satellite

UFO

Picture Dictionary 8

cook hot dogs

go canoeing

go climbing

go horseback riding

go hiking

play ball games

sing songs

tell stories

cap

compass

flashlight

map

raincoat

water bottle

26

Beep on Grammar 1

1 Complete the questions and answer for you.

1 What do __you__ have __on__ Monday? I have _____.
2 What _____ you _____ on Tuesday? _____
3 _____ do _____ have _____ Wednesday? _____
4 _____ do _____ have _____ Thursday? _____
5 What _____ _____ _____ after school today? _____

2 Read and circle the answers for you.

In my school, *we have / we don't have* a different teacher for English and math.
We have / We don't have two playgrounds.
We have / We don't have a big gym.
We have / We don't have a vegetable garden.
We have / We don't have a science laboratory.
We have / We don't have a special school song.

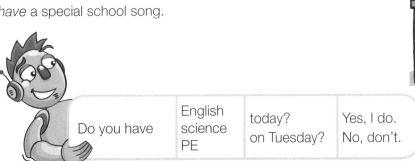

3 Complete the questions and answer *Yes, I do. / No, I don't*.

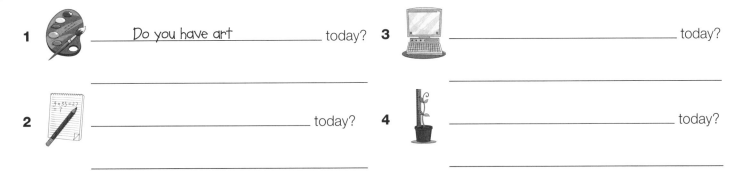

1 __Do you have art__ today?
2 _____ today?
3 _____ today?
4 _____ today?

27

Beep on Grammar 2

1 Look and write the answers.

2 Write in order and write the name.

1 speak / English / I / Spanish / and

_____. My name's _____.

2 French / and / I / Chinese / speak

_____. My name's _____.

3 and / Spanish / I / Italian / speak

_____. My name's _____.

28

Beep on Grammar 3

1 Complete the questions and answer for you.

1 _____ do _____ wear in _____ ?   January   you   What
   I wear _____.

2 _____ do you _____ _____ August?   in   Where   go
   _____

3 _____ do _____ wear _____ June?   in   you   What
   _____

4 _____ _____ you _____ _____ Christmas?   eat   on   What   do
   _____

2 Write in order and circle *True* or *False* for you.

1 I / go / August / to / In / don't / beach / the
   _____ True   False

2 June / I / a / wear / T-shirt / In
   _____ True   False

3 soccer / In / play / January / don't / I
   _____ True   False

4 soup / eat / December / In / I
   _____ True   False

3 Complete the sentences for you.

1 In spring, I _____.
2 I don't _____ in summer.
3 I _____ in autumn.
4 In winter, I don't _____.

29

Beep on Grammar 4

1 Write the questions and answer for your city, town or village.

1 Is there a train station?

2 _____

3 _____

4 _____

5 _____

6 _____

2 Write sentences, look and circle *True* or *False*.

1 swimming pool / a / There / isn't
_____ True   False

2 a / There's / train station
_____ True   False

3 movie theater / a / There's
_____ True   False

4 isn't / hospital / There / a
_____ True   False

5 a / isn't / shopping mall / There
_____ True   False

6 museum / There's / a
_____ True   False

30

Beep on Grammar 5

1 Complete the questions and answer.

1. How much is the salad? _It's three dollars and twenty cents._
2. How _____ is _____ rice? _____
3. _____ _____ is the ham? _____
4. How much _____ _____ burger? _____
5. _____ much _____ the cereal? _____

2 Write and circle for Richard.

breakfast	lunch	dinner
cereal	soup	fish
toast	salad	vegetables

1. I evah sotat rof nernid
   I have toast for dinner. True False

2. I ahev dalas rfo nluch
   _____ True False

3. I veah tabgevesel fro fabrestak
   _____ True False

4. I heav opus rfo nnride
   _____ True False

5. I aehv leerac orf kabrestaf
   _____ True False

6. I ahev sfhi ofr nulch
   _____ True False

31

Beep on Grammar 6

| They | have
don't have | legs.
wings.
antennae. |

1 Look and complete.

1 _____ wings.   4 _____ legs.   7 _____ hands.
2 _____ a stinger.   5 _____ antennae.   8 _____ claws.
3 _____ antennae.   6 _____ a stinger.   9 _____ hair.

2 Write about dragonflies.

_____
_____
_____

| How many | wings
antennae
legs | do | ladybugs
worms
bees | have? |

3 Complete the questions and answer. Look at the key and check.

1 How _____ wings _____ grasshoppers _____ ?
2 _____ _____ legs do _____ _____ ?

3 _____ many eyes _____ spiders _____ ?
4 How _____ antennae _____ spiders _____ ?

1) 4 2) 6 3) 8 4) 8 5) 6 6) 2

5 _____ _____ legs do _____ have ?
6 How _____ eyes do ladybugs _____ ?

32

Beep on Grammar 7

1.00	have lunch
3.30	take photos
2.00	write e-mails
7.00	have dinner
8.30	listen to music

1 Write questions and answer.

1 she / dinner / Does / at / 7:00 / ? / have _____ _____
2 photos / take / at / ? / Does / 4:30 / she _____ _____
3 write / 2:00 / she / e-mails / ? / Does / at _____ _____
4 lunch / 1:30 / ? / she / at / have / Does _____ _____
5 music / at / ? / 9:30 / she / to / Does / listen _____ _____

2 Look and complete.

	🎵	📖	📷
Saturday	✓	✓	✓
Sunday	✓	✗	✗

1 Malena doesn't read books on _____.
2 She _____ to music on _____ and Sunday.
3 _____ _____ photos _____ Saturday.
4 She _____ books _____ _____.
5 She _____ take _____ on Sunday.

33

Beep on Grammar 8

| I want
I don't want | to | go canoeing.
play ball games.
go climbing.
go hiking. |

1 Look and complete.

1. I want to play ball games. ✓
2. ✗
3. ✗
4. ✓

2 Write about your summer vacation plans.

1. _____ sing songs.
2. _____ go hiking.
3. _____ swim in the ocean.
4. _____ go horseback riding.
5. _____ tell stories.
6. _____ play ball games.

Track List

Student's Book
Songs, chants and stories

Track	Transcript	
Unit 0		
1	0.1	Song: Here we are in school again!
Unit 1		
2	1.1	Song: It's time for school!
3	1.4	Story: Late for School!
4	1.5	Song: Here's our classroom!
5	1.6	Beep's World!
Unit 2		
6	2.1	Song: The Countries Rap!
7	2.4	Story: The Concert!
8	2.6	Beep's World!
Unit 3		
9	3.3	Story: The Snow Monster!
10	3.4	Song: Seasons come, seasons go!
11	3.6	Beep's World!
Unit 4		
12	4.1	Song: My Town!
13	4.5	Story: The Science Museum!
14	4.7	Beep's World!
Unit 5		
15	5.1	Song: Are you hungry?
16	5.3	Story: The School Fair!
17	5.5	Beep's World!
Unit 6		
18	6.1	Song: Minibeasts are everywhere!
19	6.5	Story: The Giant Australian Treefly!
20	6.6	Beep's World!
Unit 7		
21	7.1	Song: I want to be an astronaut!
22	7.4	Story: The UFO!
23	7.6	Beep's World!
Unit 8		
24	8.1	Song: Summer Camp
25	8.5	Story: The Rescue!
26	8.7	Beep's World!

Activity Book
Exercises

Track	Transcript	
27	0.1	Listen and complete.
28	1.1	Listen and match.
29	2.1	Listen and number.
30	3.1	Listen and match.
31	4.1	Listen and check or cross.
32	5.1	Listen and write the prices.
33	6.1	Listen and complete the chart. Write the name of the minibeasts.
34	7.1	Listen and check or cross.
35	8.1	Listen and complete the chart.

Picture Dictionary

Track	Transcript	
36	PD1	Picture Dictionary 1
37	PD2	Picture Dictionary 2
38	PD3	Picture Dictionary 3
39	PD4	Picture Dictionary 4
40	PD5	Picture Dictionary 5
41	PD6	Picture Dictionary 6
42	PD7	Picture Dictionary 7
43	PD8	Picture Dictionary 8